Table of Contents

I0503812

This is Personal.

I must learn

How to

Forgive myself for

Everything I have not

Done

While I was worrying

About other

People.

I must

Stop

Expecting things

From people around

Me,

And truly level up.

This Me

I had to deal with.

Years

Of feeling

Inadequate,

Not worthy,

Ugly,

And

Invisible.

I have been in some of the deepest

And darkest

Depressions,

And

I blame myself for

Thinking that I was ever

Going to glue

My family together,

Or That my father

Ever genuinely loved

Me.

He did not even know

Me.

I must learn that

This pain

Is the building block

For me.

I must learn

That loving me

Also means loving

You.

Regardless of the way that

You

Made me feel.

This. Is. Personal.

I must understand

That you were not the

Easiest pill

To swallow

BUT,

2

You taught me more than I could

Ever Grasp

And loved me

Enough to let you go.

Affirmations.

I am

Impeccably amazing.

My black skin,

A reminder

That God himself kisses

Me with melanin.

A reminder that

I am the

Mother Land's wildest dreams.

I am

Shea butter baby and cocoa butter

Kisses.

I am

Ray - Elle, but spelled differently.

A reminder that the sun

Exists every day.

I am

The daughter of the King

Of kings.

I am full of unmasked

Talents that no one

Knew or understood.

I am not to

Be Understood.

I am

A Divine creation.

I am

More than what they tell me I am,

More than who I think I am.

I am

Beautiful in every

Curve,

Every Curl,

Every Kink.

I am

A Black woman.

I am

The most disrespected

And the most

Resilient.

I am

Breaking Generational Curses,

And

Doing it with Grace.

I am

The blueprint and the finished

Product,

I am

Under pressure.

I am

The diamond in the rough.

I am

Who he says I am!

Crowned in confidence

I am

ME!

And will always be.

Process

I can't process death anymore.

My body is physically

Numb.

I can't seem to

Understand

That someone is actually

Gone.

I want to send a text, but

They aren't

Here

Anymore.

I want a hug.

It would mean the world right

Now.

I don't know how to process

Death.

I know that we all go,

Even those we love the most.

But,

How am I supposed to just

Let them

Hurt,

And not want to take their pain away?

I can't understand why God took them

Away.

I can't understand why they would

Leave.

Call me selfish.

I wouldn't want others to feel pain.

I just wish that God could take the pain away

Without taking you.

When I lost you,

It felt like I lost a chunk of me.

Without your company,

Your smile,

Your life.

I couldn't process your

Passing because I wanted

You to be here with me.

Never,

In a thousand years, did I expect you

To leave this world

Without me.

Lord, please tell me it's a joke.

Or that you and the angels

Just playin' games.

Or that you can do

Like you did to Lazarus,

And raise them up

Again.

It's selfish of me,

But I still feel numb.

I can never forget the type

Of person that you were.

The amazing things you did

And the legacy you left.

Nothing in this world prepared me

For you to leave me.

So, I try

To carry you with me.

I try to make sure that

You know

You had your flowers

While you lived.

I can't process death anymore.

My body can't physically understand

That you're actually,

Fully and forever,

Gone.

The Kind of Pain I'm In

I never really spoke about

My pain.

The kind of pain that

Keeps you in bed because

The insides of your body

Never ceases to stop fighting itself.

The kind of pain that makes you

Try to get up in the morning,

But accept defeat,

And then, roll over and cry.

It's the kind of pain

That I must mask in order to

Do what I do.

The kind of pain

That no one thinks is real,

But you know it's there.

The kind of pain that makes you wanna

Run to hospitals,

Where you know you're going to get

Turned away for your skin tone,

Or get treated like you're addicted to pills.

It's a kind of pain that makes warriors **weak**.

It feels like multiple daggers stabbing,

Elephants stomping, and getting

Hit by a bus, all at once.

It is the kind of pain that

Band aids are not big enough to fix.

It is the kind of pain I feel,

Even on vacation.

The kind of pain that makes me snap at those I love,

And one that no one takes seriously.

The one that no one seems to care about.

The kind of pain that I have zero will to move

Because I can't feel my legs.

The worst kind of pain feels like someone

Is tearing me apart.

It's a kind of pain

That only women know.

That kind of pain.

A kind of pain

That makes you hate everything.

It's the kind of pain I'm in

A kind of pain that needs to be understood.

Taken seriously.

It's really no joke.

It's the pain that I just can't shake.

JUSTICE

It took 182.5 days to receive Justice

For the wall in Breonna Taylor's

House.

There are 525,600 minutes in

One year.

We spent 262,800 of them

Fighting for the Justice

Of Breonna Taylor.

In wake, we lost more black lives.

When will mothers stop having

To bury their babies,

Wives stop having to witness

The killing of their black husbands,

And children taking L's

On the lives of parents who stood for them.

We spent 262,800 minutes

Fighting on the main lines

In the center of a Pandemic.

SAY HER NAME!

The spray painted

BLACK LIVES MATTER

On streets, but the devil

Works hard.

But, when they go low,

We go high.

When they try to hurt us,

We will keep pushing for Justice.

We will because we did

When we said yes to

Change.

We said yes for the right to

Educate

When we put a Black Man

In the Presidential seat.

We were so set to change.

Instead of jokes,

Let's talk Justice.

Let's get Justice for Breonna Taylor,

For the countless black women

Who lost their lives to police

Brutality.

Let's take our entire

525,600 minutes, while we are alive,

To change the world that we live In.

For The children,

For the mothers,

And for the streets.

Oh and

ARREST THE KILLERS OF BREONNA TAYLOR!

AND ELIJAH MCCLAIN!

AND COUNTLESS OTHERS!

AND DON'T STOP UNTIL

THERE IS JUSTICE!

DON'T STOP BELIEVING THAT YOUR VOICE

DOESN'T COUNT!

YOU MATTER!

OUR CHILDREN MATTER!

BLACK LIVES MATTER!

How I Almost Lost You

You filled my stratosphere.

Your heart

Felt in tune with mine.

Your breath

Mimicked mine.

So perfectly, we buried

The pain that we felt

To mimic happiness.

We allowed the facade of

Perfection

To cloud our thoughts.

That the filter came off

And,

I

Hated

You.

I hated you for going behind my back.

I hated you for making me feel

Inadequate.

I hated you because you challenged me

To believe.

You forced me to pray for you

More than I had before.

You made me look at my own

Faults.

I hated the burning thought of being

hypocritical and leaving you.

I hated you.

I hated me.

I hated God...

How can I run into your Kingdom,

And you do such catastrophic things in my relationships?

How dare you take full

Permission to turn my world

UPSIDE DOWN

And

UPSET MY WORLD

After I purposefully prayed that same prayer?

How could I hate God?

He only answered my prayer...

And here you are vulnerable,

And here I am

Angry.

Smoke coming out of the ears

And all I can do Is

EXTEND GRACE

because

Losing you wouldn't make me feel better.

It'd only make me feel worse.

I would only amount to texting you a thousand times a day.

And running to your house

Looking crazy.

Because I would've made the worst

mistake

of my life,

If I ever lost you...

I would have

Lost

The very Essence

Of your

Soul.

I'd miss you,

Making it a point to love you

Even when you could honestly walk away!

I never want you

To walk

Away.

I almost lost the soul

To my

Soulmate,

The Boaz to my Ruth.

I hated myself because I

Loved you,

And everything we went

Through.

We played hide and seek.

The enemy tried to

Get between us.

He said let me plant

The seed of

Porn

Into your lives and see if you

Really love her.

Love Him.

Love us.

I will never give up on this

Rock.

We made it through love.

We pressed on.

We manifest.

We kept growing.

What the enemy thought

Was gonna end us,

Made us stronger.

On fire.

One together.

God is gonna use this

For his glory.

We are more than

Anything the enemy

Ever does.

Because ABBA

Conquered it all.

And

I Will

NEVER

LOSE

YOU

AGAIN!

FRI

The prefix Fri follows in the footsteps

As the word Free,

Meaning unconstrained,

Not imprisoned,

Released.

To be free is to set your soul apart,

So that others can truly see the

God in You.

They can see the authority in you,

so that they can

Pick up their jar of freedom.

Fri doesn't hold anything back

Just because she wants to.

She throws her punches.

Fri is the Wild Card.

She might not always show up.

But, every time she does,

She constantly keeps order.

Fri is the beginning.

She isn't ashamed to

Tell the truth.

End

The word end means the final

Pit stop. It never

Continues.

To end things is to be

Strong in God's timing.

Everything good comes to an end.

The beauty will fade,

Life as we know it

Is gone.

The end of seasons

Warrants the change

In the leaves.

What lessons to take

And which one to leave.

Every good thing

Really has to end,

For a season that is.

When God ordains the end,

Wait for the start of a new

Beginning.

He would never let us fail

When it's his plan!

FRIEND

I don't do great making new friends.

I just don't.

I tend to be awkward.

I tend to get

Far too

Comfortable.

I tend to say the wrong things.

As a friend, I can be

Too much.

To know your goals,

Spiritually,

Mentally,

Physically,

Financially,

Can be draining.

I am a weirdo, and I say things

I don't mean.

I try to make it fun, but I'm really just

Annoying.

I can sometimes get too clingy

And jealous when my friends

Have other friends.

I just wanna be your friend.

I wanna know that I'm good

Enough.

That I can hold a conversation,

And still think that I am

Enough.

The Choice to Survive

Life felt like I was constantly underwater.

Hard to breathe.

Stuck.

They don't talk about it.

"JUST GET OVER IT",

They said.

Living life in a bubble.

Afraid that if someone got close,

They'd pop it.

If someone got to close,

I'd shut the door.

Leaving them to wonder,

What exactly they did to

Hurt me.

I was pushing against the currents,

Unaware that the pain that

Crippled me, would pull me

Beneath the waves.

I can't swim.

I'd flail my arms around for someone

To come see me, but

I was far too deep in the water.

Felt like I had no room to

Move.

Scared of what I may see,

Eyes closed,

I just float.

In my mind, wondering where the

Oxygen is coming from.

The sharks protect me,

The fish relax me,

The sun breaks the surface

Of the sea.

I was no longer afraid.

The whale puts me on its back,

And brings me out of the water.

Deep breaths.

Deep breaths.

The sun still shining on my

Face.

The sweet sound of the

Ocean waves comfort me

'Til I fall asleep.

The sweet aroma of salt.

Meeting the sand, a fresh aroma

In my nostrils.

Recognizing the change in

my heart.

The whale had brought

me to the

Surface.

My life was brought

Back to the surface.

Sand clinging to every unshaven

Hair on my legs.

I see the footprints in the sand.

I see the footprints in the sand.

The One that says,

"I am for you,

Not against you."

The one that says,

"I will never leave you,

Nor forsake you."

The one that says,

"I am the friend,

Closer than a brother,

The Father to the fatherless

The great I am."

I stood in the footprints.

The solidity of such sand,

It awakened my spirit.

I forgot I was wet.

I forgot the

Splendor of the Son that,

It overtook me.

When I couldn't swim,

He called the sharks to

Protect me.

When I was anxious,

He called the fish to comfort me

When he was ready to show his glory,

He put his footprint in the sand.

He put the reminder in my soul.

So that when someone got close,

They built me up.

So when someone comes close,

I no longer think about the bubble.

I no longer think about

My worth.

I no longer think about

My fears.

I think about my Father

I think about my ABBA.

I turn to him when I

Want to give up.

I turn my attention to him

When I want to get off track.

When All else failed,

He was the Anchor.

In the footprints,

I made the choice to

Survive.

I made the choice to

Come back to the who

And whose I am.

I decided to give it a brand new song.

I decided to play a new game.

I decided to move differently,
To become strong.
For when I was at the end of
My rope,
God said I
Wasn't at the end
Of His.
His grace was all I needed.
His love carried me,
Though I should've been
Gone.
His favor speaks
Even when I'm silent,
And his Joy
Becomes me after the storm.
He brought me out
The water.
And Shone his light
To make me whole
Again.
Just as he
Intended.

Talk Trauma

Abused,

Beaten,

Torn,

And Used,

At the age of 6,

My cousins and

I would play

Hide and Seek,

Hiding in closets,

Just to kiss.

I thought all cousins

Did that!

At the age of 8,

We played House.

We openly kissed,

Just to show

Mom and Dad

Loved each other.

We ended up

Embarrassed.

I thought that was

Normal.

At age 10,

We learned what fingers

Could do

From Sex Ed.

It was encouraged

To learn

Our own bodies.

At age 11,

The internet was

The playground.

Countless sleepless

Nights,

Watching

Lesbian porn.

It was just what I knew.

Age 12,

Sierra Leone,

West Africa.

Before school ends,

I was

Molested

by a classmate.

I was blamed for the

Entire

Thing.

Ass beat.

Age 13,

I spiraled into

Depression.

I hated myself.

I didn't care.

I sat alone for

Many nights

Trying to die.

Age 14,

The suicide attempt.

Took 32 pills,

Thinking I could take the pain away,

But the pain was

Still there.

Age 15,

I finally acknowledged

The eating disorder.

It caused me

To be blind to myself.

Who am I?

Age 18,

Welcome to SCAD

Undergrad.

Excited to take on

A new world.

College was the perfect

Place to be.

Except I was nowhere close

To ready.

Sexually abused at

A party,

Left me broken.

Running back home

To mama.

Then allowing

Myself

To get abused again,

On my very couch.

I wasn't ready.

I wasn't ready.

I wasn't ready.

Age 19,

Learning slowly how

To live for myself.

I met a guy,

He's pretty nice.

I hated being so empty.

He needed me too!

I was trying to find

Me.

Little did I know

Was me

Was lost.

Age 21

Legally allowed to drink.

Legally allowed to get.

The fuck

Out of my mother's house.

We fought like

Clockwork.

I resented her,

For everything she didn't

Know.

But, how could she see?

I was so closed off!

How could I

Love my mom

With the filter of

Broken on?

I hated myself,

Which made me

Hate

Everyone.

Age 22,

I found God

In a Marriott Hotel.

Locked out the house,

I had crossed the

Boundary.

I had made it clear,

That I was hurting.

I thought I lost

My Mom.

I recognized that everything

From the porn,

To the abuse,

To the eating disorder,

To the childhood trauma,

To the countless jobs I lost,

To not feeling good

Enough,

Made me bitter.

I had to mourn the losses,

And forgive the unfair.

I didn't ask to be born into

It.

But, here I was.

I was responsible to heal,

And I did.

My boyfriend taking the

Brute force

Of my passive-aggressive

My mom.

Learning how to love

Me all over again,

And me taking on the rings for myself,

God had his hand on it from the beginning,

He had his fingerprint

In it.

It has his blood on it.

2020 was his year to make

Me,

see him for who he is.

No amount of man

Could ever bring me joy the way

God has.

22 has been the toughest,

But most rewarding years

Of my life.

Age 23,

Engaged,

Happy,

Financially free,

Claiming blessings

On blessings,

A bonafide business

Owner,

And

One world

Traveler,

To see what the

Lord has done

All over!

Your story isn't over yet...

The pages are still being written...

Affirm You

You are so beautiful.

You carry light

Within you.

You love deep,

And you've been trying to

Be the best you can be.

I see you.

Your emotions are valid.

Your love

Is valid.

Who you are is valid.

They want to put things

Onto you to make them feel better.

Forget them.

Extend the grace to love them.

Take your time

To truly embrace you.

You are all together,

Amazing.

You are

Unique,

Vibrant,

Awesome,

Wonderful,

And Phenomenal.

As Ms.Angelou

Would say,

You carry so much

Potential,

The world won't ever understand.

You...

You create.

You inspire.

You encourage.

You are just enough.

You are always

Stunning,

Jaw-dropping,

Absolutely turning heads

When you walk into

A room.

They notice you.

You Are

Going to make a lot of

People proud.

I'm ecstatic to

See you grow!

Keep

Doing

You boo

FIN.

Poets Notes

In this second edition of Asylum, it truly felt like I was able to vent to you. To tell you a little bit more about myself, and share a little bit more about my faith. I have gone through some genuine ups and some very hard downs. I wanted to talk about my porn addiction so that others know that they aren't alone in whatever their addiction is. It's been a hard pill to swallow being able to heal the emotional pain that was traced directly to the trauma in my childhood. From my panic disorder to my depression, I'm airing out my own dirty laundry so that I can personally heal, and so that others reading these words will see that I never held anything back.

To the amazing future poets, I want you to write your heart out, never stop until you can feel the change within yourself. Never forget that writing and reading is therapy, and no matter what just keep swimming!

You never usually see dedications at the end of books... but

Shout out to the world's best editor in the entire world Vanessa Pham, she did the damn thing for sure!

Shoutout to the FroHaze Team cuz y'all hyped a sis up for v.2

To my mommy and my sister, I love you with all my heart

To the love of my life... I love you 3000

To everyone else! Thank you for supporting my dreams!

About the Poet

Samantha Raelle Cole aka Manii Raelle is an artist, Chanel makeup artist, designer, entrepreneur, and now an author. Poetry has always been something she's been passionate about, and she is always writing or reading. Her influences are poets Maya Angelou & Langston Hughes and novelists Toni Morrison, Tomi Adeyemi, and Jay Malik. You can find Manii talking about FroHaze, painting (digitally or traditionally), hanging out with her amazing boyfriend Mike, playing any Legend of Zelda game (anyone else obsessed?) , or watching murder mysteries shows with her mother and sister!

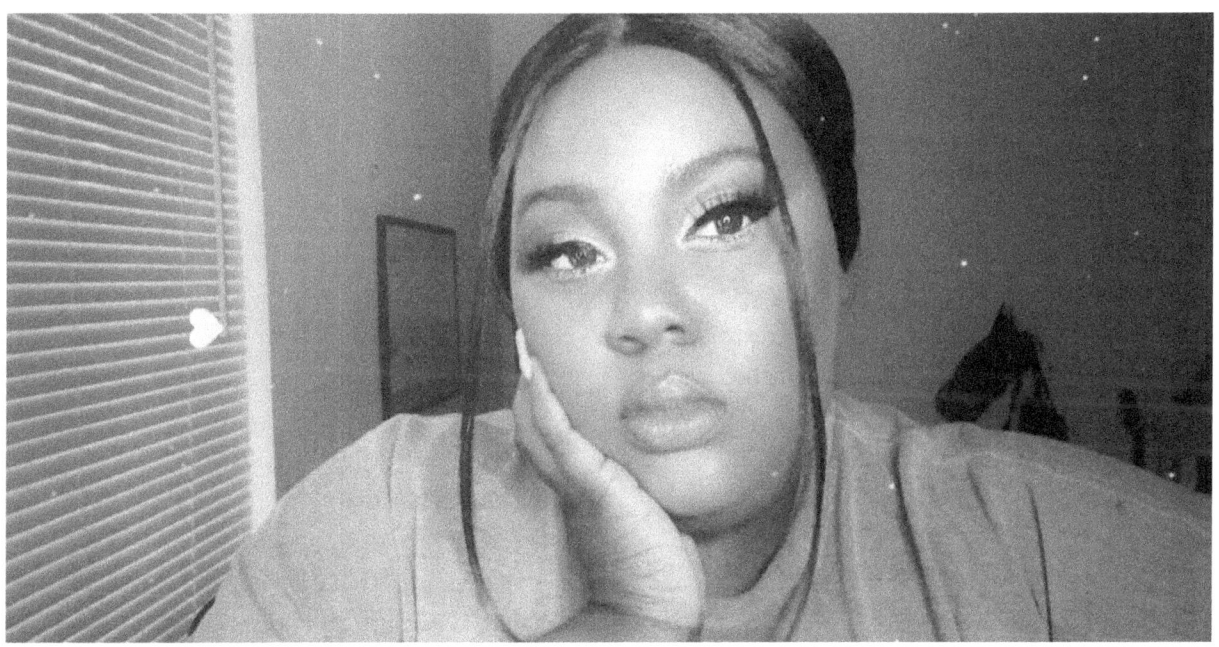